Poetry Overcomes Evil-Minded Spirits

(A collection of Faith based Poetry crafted to calm the most restless Heart)

Rain

Let the rain of love fall down on you like a flood.

Once it comes just take it to heart.

The Lords' rain is a positive encouraging rain.

Satins' rain is all full of hate.

All his rain does is keep you down.

Walking through the rain of love gives you strength.

Going through the rain of hate only makes you weak.

For me, I walk through the rain of love.

We are to fly like eagles through love.

Or you can sink in the rain of hate.

Are you going to sink or fly?

Umbrella

When the storm of life hits, it hits hard.

The storm of life does not play fair at all.

Our Lord gives us an umbrella to use.

It is up to us to take it out.

As long as we stay under it, we are protected.

Sometime we get stuck in the storm of life.

At times, we think we are invisible to the storm of life.

Then Jesus has to remind us that the storm is bigger.

The only way we can beat the storm is with His strength.

So do not let the storm choke you out.

Naturally

Just as our sin comes naturally by birth,

We have to learn how to walk in the spirit.

The spirit of Christ has to be first nature to us.

As we walk, the spirit has to lead our path.

He is our compass for the path of life.

Within us is a fire that's ever-lasting.

It lights our road called life.

The light of the spirit warms our path.

As our compass, He is always on point.

We have to keep a constant natural flow in the spirit.

The Show Goes On

Life has many challenges and difficulties.

As we go through them, Christ is over us.

The challenges of life got the best of me lately.

Keep Christ first, the show goes on smoothly.

It won't be easy, but it is worth it.

Jesus' love overrides all of life's challenges.

The show goes on as the rain of faith falls.

That's the one thing that keeps my show going.

Remember to keep the show of life going.

Don't let the show of life take advantage of you.

With Arms Wide Open

We are to come with arms wide open.

Opening our hearts to the Lord with honesty.

He wants us to come freely open.

It's up to us to be open like children.

I used to be a very closed in hard head.

It took a very special person to break the wall.

The love that was always given shaped me.

A one of a kind bond was formed.

This is a unique bond that is special.

That's how I became freely open like a child.

Take A Bow

Let's take a bow to the one and only true God.

Start worshipping him with our whole hearts.

Stop worshipping the god of this earth.

He is the cancer that kills the spirit.

It spreads like a wild fire.

The Lord Jesus comes to heal like a flood,

with the water of love to clean out the cancer.

It is a pure and holy water from above.

Satan's water is a blood bath that only causes strife.

Jesus' water brings peace and joy.

For me, I am with Jesus all the way.

Please Don't Stop the Music

Please don't stop the music deep in my heart.

That is the love which drives me to push harder.

The music in my heart comes from above.

My heart used to be a speaker without sound.

Now my heart is always on full blast.

Power from on high keeps our music at flow.

The joy of our music does not come from earthly things.

Our music joy comes from kingdom things.

Don't let the music in your heart ever stop.

That music is what drives my passion deeper.

Tattoo

There are only two types of tattoos in this dark world.

These are spiritual tattoos on the heart.

The tattoos of Christ are love, faith, and hope.

Satan's tattoos are hate, anger, and envy.

My old tattoos were hate, anger, rebellion.

Now my tattoos are love, joy, and peace.

The tattoos of Christ bring eternal life.

Tattoos from Satan brings eternal death,

so choose the tattoo's on your heart wisely.

It will cost you eternal life or death.

Shape of My Heart

The shape of our hearts shows our characteristics.

Our heart reflects the characteristics of Christ in us,

or it can reflect the characteristics of Satan.

My heart reflects the light of Christ.

It used to reflect the kingdom darkness.

So does your heart reflect Christ or Satan?

The characteristics of Christ bring a good name.

Satan's characteristics bring a bad name.

You can have love in your heart or you can let the evil crush the heart.

Breathe

It's time to breathe in the spirit of love,

or you can breathe in the spirit of hate.

I used to have a lot of hate deep inside.

Most of it going towards the world.

Now my spirit is full of love.

The spirit of love only comes from Christ.

Satan is the root cause of all hate.

You can live in love or hate.

Love gives you a peace of mind.

Hate brings you misery in life.

For me, I'm all about the spirit of love.

Cheers

Thanksgiving is a time to be thankful for friends and family.

It's the time of year to be grateful.

Life comes and goes, but family will last forever more.

So let's show our family how thankful we are.

My family and friends mean the world to me.

Let's tell them we love and appreciate what they do.

Family is a very special gift from above.

Family is very important to me.

So don't wait till it's too late.

Let's give cheers on high for having family.

Who will also confirm you to the end, that you may be blameless in the day of our Lord, Jesus Christ. God is faithful, by whom you were called into the fellowship of his son, Jesus Christ, our Lord. - 1 Corinthians 1:8,9 (New King James Version)

Where Are You Christmas

Christmas is the time when family gather together into the fellowship of the King of kings.

When we celebrate the birth of King Jesus Christ.

This world doesn't know where the word Christmas came from.

There is a deeper meaning to the word Christmas.

The root word in Christmas is Christ.

King Jesus Christ shows us what Christmas is about.

Christmas isn't about just getting stuff.

It's about giving back to others.

That is what Jesus Christ taught us to do.

For the wages of sin is death, but the gift of God is eternal life in Christ Jesus, our Lord.
- Romans 6:23 (New King James Version)

Eyes Open

We need to keep our eyes open on the battlefield of life.

The battlefield of life all starts in the mind.

My battlefield is with myself.

At one point my eyes were closed to the battlefield.

Too many peoples' eyes are spiritually closed.

This battlefield called life is not easy at all.

We need to fight through the battle of life, in order to stay strong in our faith.

Our faith is what builds our strength for battle.

That is what keeps me fighting on.

So let's keep the strong faith of courage.

Fight the good fight of faith, joy hold on eternal life, to which you were also called and have confessed the good confession in the presence of many witnesses. -1 Timothy 6:12 (New king James Version)

Break Away

We need to break away from the old lifestyle.

It is like an old stain on the soul that we collected over the years.

The blood of Christ washes out every stain.

He has the purest bleach out there.

Jesus Christ washes us as white as snow.

There is not a stain he can't get out.

The stain is our past lifestyle.

All we can do is look forward to the future.

We will still have our shortcomings.

Jesus still loves us any way.

Purge me with hyssop, and I shall be clean, wash me, and I shall be whiter than snow   -
Psalms 51:7 (New King James Version)

Soldiers of Faith

As soldiers of faith we overcome through Christ Jesus.

We are lifelong soldiers for Christ.

Let's walk this year out with faith.

Christ Jesus perfects our faith as we stay the course.

Challenges will come to test our level of faith.

We are to fly high in the sky like eagles.

I fly free as an eagle through the sky.

This is the year we will walk in courageous faith

So, let us stay strong in the army of Christ Jesus.

Keep the faith going strong.

Let no one despise your youth, but be an example to the believers in word, in conduct, in love, in spirit, in faith, in purity.- 1 Timothy 4:12(New King James Version)

Irreplaceable

Great-grandma there's no one else like you in this world.

You are truly one of a kind in my life.

Your love has always been in my heart.

The love you have is something special to me.

Great-grandma you have always meant the world to me.

There is no one more special than you in my life.

You will always be the second special lady in my life.

My love for you is far beyond this world.

Your love will always remain in my heart forever.

Thank you for always being there.

Teardrops On My Guitar

From the day I first saw you,

You are a very special lady.

You are the reason I cry teardrops of joy.

Without you I wouldn't be the person I am today.

My love will never change for you.

It was just under a lot of anger.

The love I have will always be there.

You will always be the special lady in my life.

Mother, you are the reason for the teardrops on my guitar.

Whoever robs their father and drives out their mother is a child who brings shame and disgrace. Stop listening to instruction, my son, and you will stray from the words of knowledge.- Proverbs 19:26-27 (New King James Version)

Walking On Water

Walking on water is going all out by faith.

Going out by faith takes full trust in Christ.

Faith is going to take us out of our comfort zone.

We have to step out farther to grow our faith.

Stepping out in faith takes a strong courage.

Christ is the one who strengthens our faith.

Faith is believing in the unseen.

It takes faith to walk on spiritual water.

Deeper the water, more faith it takes to stand firm.

Christ wants us to stand firm in our faith.

Whoever believes in me, as scripture has said, rivers of living water will flow from within them.
John 7:38 (New King James Version)

Sparks Fly

Love sparks free like a bird high in the sky.

Sparks fly everywhere throughout the air.

The most powerful spark is love.

Love is a force that always wins in the end.

Jesus' love always has the final word.

Hate is a force that's a sore loser.

She is a powerful force that overcomes all things.

It breaks down any wall we have up.

Loves presence wants to overflow within us.

The presence of love is the greatest friend ever.

Red

Red is the sacrificial color of love.

The sacrifice of love was Jesus Christ.

We have life through the risen King Christ.

Black is the color of death.

Satan comes to take away life.

Life with Christ gives eternal life.

Living with Satan brings eternal torment.

Love brings an abundant life to all.

Risen King will never leave you.

He watches over all of his children.

His love surpasses above all things.

Love is a sacrificial action we make.

Jesus made a sacrificial action for us.

We may abandon love but love doesn't abandon us.

Love says I have always believed in you.

We had to get connected with love first.

She is the greatest friend I can ask for.

The king is waiting to be your everlasting friend.

Jesus wants to fill you with his eternal love.

He says come as you are my child.

You have nothing to fear with me, my son.

My love looks beyond all past mistakes.

The presence of love forgives all.

She is saying forgive yourself.

Everlasting Friend

Love is an everlasting friend that never fails on us.

She is a friend you can always count on.

We didn't find love, she found us.

Love has been waiting for us to open the door and our hearts.

Her Touch always stays soft and gentle,

Like a mother who comforts her child.

That's how love is with us.

As a friend, she is trust worthy.

She sticks closer than a sister.

Just like a sister, she is always there for you.

Her arms are always wide open.

Let all that you do be done in love - 1 Corinthians 16:14 (New King James Version)

Baseball of Faith

Faith is like baseball, slow but steady.

We have to keep faithful and steady walking in faith.

Faith is walking in something we can't see.

We just have trust in it and believe.

First base is your study time.

Dig in and study for yourself.

Next, second base is prayer time.

Pour your whole heart out to the heavenly father.

Lastly, third base is the application in our walk.

The most important one of them all.

Without the application the other two don't work.

Remember prayer is our source of strength.

Then the word is the food we eat.

Application is the key source in the bowl.

I can do everything through Christ who gives me strength - Philippians 4:13 (New King James Version)

Dreaming of You

Robin, you are a dream on my heart forever.

Memories of you are the star on my heart.

Your love is a river flowing through my heart.

Words can't express how much you mean to me.

Robin, I am thankful for having you.

You were always a special lady in my life.

Robin, your love will always be remembered.

Your love will always be in my heart.

Nothing can replace your tender caring for me.

No one can take your place as number one aunt.

RIP Robin

Life

So many of us take life for an advantage.

Life is a very special gift from the almighty one.

We have this gift for purpose in life.

This gift is no game to play with.

Life is a one-shot gift we have.

Let's not waste time on foolish things.

So let's live life in a peaceful way.

The gift of life is so precious to us.

Life is the most beautiful thing we have.

Let's stop complaining and be grateful for what we do have.

Life is short so let's make the best of it while we can.

Very Special Lady

Mother, you have been the special lady in my life from the beginning.

You're the first one to hold me in your arms.

Without you I wouldn't be the person I am today.

I thank you for always believing in me.

You will always be the first lady in my life.

There is no other special lady than you.

Your love is the key to my gentle heart.

There is no better friend than a mother.

You have always meant the world to me.

Happy Mother's Day to a very special lady.

Champion

We are champions through Christ all the time.

As champions we have the strength in us to overcome.

Like an eagle, spread our wings and fly.

With Christ as our eagle eyes.

Champions have Christ Jesus fighting their battles.

Being a champion is like flying first-class.

The strength in us allows us to surpass the impossible.

As champions, we have a true peace of mind.

Champions have a fearless fire, deep inside of them.

That fire is everlasting, burning inside of us.

Every Where

Grandma, you are everywhere deep in my heart.

You will always be in my heart forever more.

There is no other special grandma like you.

You will always be my number one angel.

You're the one that understands me the best.

We are alike in so many ways.

There is no other friend like you.

Everywhere I go, you are always with me.

You have always been my open ears.

No one else can take your place as my close friend.

There is only enough room in this world for one special grandma.

That is, you.

Love, your number one grandson.

God Must Have Spent a Little More Time On You

Tyler, you are truly a blessing in my little life.

You will always be my buddy for life.

God made you special, the way you are,

So, don't let anybody tell you different.

You're a bright and shining gift from heaven.

Tyler, you are a very sharp young man.

No one can replace you as my little buddy.

Tyler, you have always brightened up my day.

You are my bright and shining star.

So, keep on shining little buddy.

All You Wanted

All you wanted was a friend you can always count on.

A friend that will always have your back.

When you feel like no one cares.

Trust me, I used to feel the same way.

So, you are not alone there, my friend.

Then I found Jesus, the greatest friend ever.

He is the only one that can fill the emptiness.

Jesus wants to be the friend you always wanted.

That's a friend you can always come to anytime.

He is always open to listen to us.

This is a friend that won't let you down.

By Richie Sweitzer

Battle Scars

Pastor Jacoby, you were the first one to show me love.

You loved me for who I was.

That is something I will never ever forget.

Pastor Jacoby, you have made a huge impact in my life.

I wouldn't be where I am today without you.

You have made a huge impact on others.

Pastor Jacoby, you will always be loved.

You were like a dad to me.

No one made me feel welcomed like you did.

RIP Pastor Jacoby.

By Richie Sweitzer

Fear Less

Love gives us the power to be fearless leaders.

Faith is the strength that keeps us going strong.

Hope is our light that shines bright.

We're called to be fearless leaders in this world.

We are the lighthouse in this dark world.

Love is what makes a fearless leader truly different.

Not all Leaders are fearless.

The love of Christ is what empowers us to be fearless leaders.

For me, love changes everything about leadership.

Love is the most important thing in leading.

I would like to dedicate this to brothers Kurt, Rome, Jack and Tom.

By Richie Sweitzer

The Way You Love Me

Grandma, your love has always been the same for me.

You still loved me when I was acting childish.

Even when I was hurtful, you still showed me compassion.

Your love is like arms wrapped around my heart.

Nothing can ever take that feeling away from me.

You will always be the first special lady in my life.

No one else can take that spot.

Without your love I would have given up.

You loved me for who I was.

Words can't express how I feel.

I'm very grateful to have you as my number one grandma.

You're not just my number one grandma.

You are my number one friend.

By Richie Sweitzer.

Love, your Number One Grandson.

Come on Over

Come on over to the spirit of love and truth.

It's a choice you will not regret.

So, stop fighting the spirit of truth.

He only wants to help you live a better life.

The spirit of love says, come as you are.

It does not matter what you have been through.

I love you for who you are, my child.

My love for you is beyond understanding.

The spirit of love comes freely.

He doesn't force himself on us.

So, follow the spirit of love with forgiveness.

Forgiveness goes with the spirit of love.

By Richie Sweitzer

My Beautiful Special Mother

Happy Birthday to a very beautiful special mother.

No one else can take your place as my beautiful mother.

Without you, I wouldn't be the man I am today.

You will always be my first special lady.

Nothing can replace my feelings for you, mother.

There is no other mother like you in this world.

You're my only top lady in this world.

Nothing can change what we have.

You will forever be my beautiful special mother.

By Richie Sweitzer

Change

So many people think change comes from the outside in.

Change comes from the inside out.

This process is walking the walk,

Not just talking the talk.

With change comes some sacrifice.

Sacrifice to self and old ways.

Take it from someone whose been there.

Change is not going to be easy.

You have to trust the process of change.

Picture it like learning how to ride a bike.

Change is about taking it slow and steady.

You cannot control the process of change.

We just have to walk with the process.

The process of change takes full total trust.

By Richie Sweitzer

Gone But Always in My Heart

This goes out to all the 9/11 victims and families.

Their pain and loss will be remembered always.

This is a time we should remember the Pledge of Allegiance.

What the meaning behind it means any more.

Has America forgot what it means to be an American.

To all of those who suffered, you're always in my heart.

That was a terrible day for America.

We should take a moment to remember those victims.

So, let us remember what it means to be an American.

By Richie Sweitzer

Every Man's Struggle

Every man struggles with lust in some way.

Lust comes in many different forms.

It has its own way with each man.

Lust is like a spiritual cold.

Our daily remedy is study and prayer.

This our only source to remain strong.

We can't light this on our own.

That is like going to war without a gun.

You can't hide or run lust at all.

Face it, lust is everywhere we go.

This also applies to my daily battle.

So, don't think you're alone in this.

And those who belong in Christ Jesus have crucified the flesh with its passions and desires.
-Galatians 5:24 (New King James Version)

By Richie Sweitzer

Never Ending Love

Great-grandma, your love has never failed me.

You have always been by my side.

Your love was always there to comfort me.

You will always be my second special lady.

There is no other great grandma like you in this world.

You have been the best great-grandma ever.

No other great grandma can love me like you do.

You're not just my great-grandma.

You're my best friend.

So Happy Birthday to a very special lady.

Grandchildren are the crown of the aged, and the glory of children is their fathers.
- Proverbs 17:6 (New King James Version)

By Richie Sweitzer

Over and Over Again

Grandma and grandpa, you have loved me over and over again.

Many of times as I hurt you guys.

Nothing will change what you did for me.

You two will always be my special grandparents.

My love has always been there for you two.

It was under a lot of anger and hate.

Words can't express my love for you guys.

Both of you have helped me through a lot growing up.

I am truly grateful for the both of you.

Thank you for always believing in me.

You guys are the best grandparents.

Above all, keep loving one another earnestly, since love covers a multitude of sins. 1 Peter 4:8 (New King James Version)

By Richie Sweitzer

I'm With You

Even when we slip off the path of Jesus,

Jesus is saying I am waiting for you.

Yes, your one and only Richie, slipped off that path.

To all of those who fell off, there's still hope.

Take it from me, that's getting back to Jesus.

So stop feeling bad and take the steps.

Feeling bad is going to hold back the process.

That was holding me back.

If you are ashamed of what happened, so was I for a while.

Jesus sees beyond all that through love.

You are not alone on the path back to Jesus.

For the righteous falls seven times and rises again, but the wicked stumble in times of calamity.
- Proverbs 24:16 (New King James Version)

By Richie Sweitzer

Smile

As leaders, we put on a smile to stay strong.

Even when we are hurting or struggling.

Most of the time I hide it behind a smile.

Behind that smile I am going through something.

A smile can cover many things.

At the same time, they are powerful.

They can brighten someone's day.

So many people have frowns on their faces.

Let's learn how to smile more often.

One smile can go a long way.

These things I have spoken to you, that in me, you may have peace. In the world, you will have tribulation; but be of good cheer, I have overcome the world. - John 16:33 (New King James Version)

By Richie Sweitzer

Importance of Family

Family is like a body working together,

like staying in good health.

That is how important a family relationship is.

The beginning of life is about family.

Family is the beginning of new adventures in life.

Love from family is a very special gift.

The greatest gift ever is family.

We may have different roles in the picture.

In the end, family always wins.

Let's remember what the importance of family means.

Happy Thanksgiving everybody.

A devout man who feared God with all of his household, gave alms generously to the people, and prayed continually to God.- Acts 10:2 (New King James Version)

By Richie Sweitzer

One of A Kind Gift

Love is a gift that touches the heart from the inside out.

This gift comes from above.

She is tender and gentle.

Love is a sacrifice.

It shows compassion to others.

Love has a deeper meaning than words.

We have to show it in our actions towards others.

She teaches us how to forgive others.

Love accepts us for who we are.

Love shows us how to treat others.

Love is patient and kind; love does not envy or boast; it is not arrogant or rude. It does not insist on its own way; it is not irritable or resentful; it does not rejoice at wrong doing, but rejoices with the truth. Love bears all things, believe all things, hopes all things, endures all things.
- 1 Corinthians 13:4-7 (New King James version)

By Richie Sweitzer

Wildest Dreams

Dreams keep us looking towards the future.

They keep me striving harder.

We have to speak our dreams in the atmosphere.

All dreams are possible with faith.

Always keep your eye on the prize.

That is the success of your dream.

No dream is too hard for the Lord.

We have to keep our focus on Him.

I can do all things through Christ who strengthens me. - Philippians 4:13 (New King James Version)

By Richie Sweitzer

I Turn to You

You have always been the best comforter ever.

Even when I was stuck on myself.

Your love always kept me going on.

Love is always knocking at the door.

She understands your pain and hurt.

Her gentle arms are always open with your love.

I made it through hard times.

Thanks to you I can share my story.

But God shows his love for us in that while we were still sinners, Christ died for us.
- Romans 5:8 (New King James Version)

By Richie Sweitzer

Just Like Fire

We all have a fire deep within us.

You have to find what fuels your fire.

That fire can inspire someone else.

Which can spark their own fire.

This fire is your passion.

The fuel is what drives your passion.

My fuel is helping others and changing lives.

Just like fire, our passion can change things,

So, are you ready to make a difference?

The last thing that drives me is family.

By Richie Sweitzer

My Beautiful and Sweet Mother

Happy Mother's Day to a sweet and gentle lady.

Your loving touch will always comfort me.

You will always be my beautiful and sweet lady.

Mom, you make me feel special inside.

Around you, I am free as a bird.

You are a fun mom to be around.

There is no other mom like you in this world.

Happy Mother's Day to a special and understanding lady.

By Richie Sweitzer

My Beautiful and Sweet Aunt

Robin, Happy Mother's Day to a sweet and caring lady.

You helped me see the best in myself.

Thank you for pulling the best out of me.

Without you, I wouldn't see the best in me today.

Happy Mother's Day to a very special and loving aunt.

Robin, you are the best aunt in the world.

There was no other aunt like you, Robin.

Your caring touch will always be remembered.

This one is for you, Robin RIP.

By Richie Sweitzer

Stronger

We are stronger than our emotions in us.

Lately, my feelings been thinking about my mother.

Everything hitting me like a huge wave.

All the pain coming as a stabbing knife to the head.

The love of Christ heals all pain.

Jesus strengthens our pain with his comfort.

He comforts us with his loving, open arms.

Telling me that I am his loved son,

who he is very proud to have.

His love keeps me going on strong.

By Richie Sweitzer

Power of Music

The power of music can uplift or encourage.

Music has an influence to inspire or express self.

For some it is a way to escape.

I used to find escape through music.

My inspiration comes through music.

Music can change one's mindset.

It can make one pursue their dreams.

Power of music affects everyone different.

The effects of music are very influential to the mind.

By Richie Sweitzer

Real Music

Music is something that you feel within you.

The feeling of music comes from the heart.

You should be able to express yourself through music.

Music takes me to my own world.

It is something you feel flowing through you.

The rhythm will come to you naturally.

You should be able to feel what the artist feels.

The best masterpiece comes from what is in the heart.

Music takes me to a state of peace.

Real music sends a message.

It lets you express yourself freely.

By Richie Sweitzer

A Woman's Beauty

A woman's beauty is like looking into a diamond.

You see what makes her special inside.

Her true beauty comes from within.

Their love is a priceless gift.

Being surrounded under their wings of comfort.

That is what makes a woman truly beautiful.

Their beauty is not only about looks.

Having a special lady is the best feeling.

Their beauty is gentle as a flower.

They are the sweetest thing in life.

A woman's beauty is like art work.

By Richie Sweitzer

Picture to Burn

The old me is like ashes in the ground.

Those ashes flew like the wind.

Which was my spiral downfall.

Where my eyes fell off of Jesus.

Finally coming back to my senses,

seeing how far I drifted off.

Now that my eyes are back on the Prize

My past is a picture to burn.

Sometimes we may fall down.

But that shouldn't keep us in the dirt.

Just look at my story.

You're not alone if you are down in the dirt.

For the righteous falls seven times and rises again, but the wicked stumble in times of calamity.
- Proverbs 24:16 (New King James Version)

By Richie Sweitzer

Damaged

Even though I have been through a lot growing up,

 I wouldn't change any part of it.

That helped me become who I am today.

Showed me what not to be like.

Trust me, my heart has been damaged too.

Take it from someone who has been down the road.

I had my share of hurt and pain in life.

It helped make me a strong and independent young man.

That hurt and pain groomed me to who I am today.

Despise it all, I wouldn't change a thing.

And we know that all things work together for good to those who love God, to those who are the called according to his purpose. - Romans 8:28 (New King James Version)

By Richie Sweitzer

Mean

Sometimes life throws a curve ball at us.

The world is the curve ball.

Trying to make us stumble.

Wanting to see us fail in life.

Our mighty bat of truth is Jesus Christ.

With the bat we can knock the ball out.

That bat is our daily strength we need.

As long as we stay focused on Jesus Christ.

But to him who does not work but believes on him who justifies the unholy, his faith is accounted for righteousness. - Romans 4:5 (New King James Version)

By Richie Sweitzer

www.ingramcontent.com/pod-product-compliance
Lightning Source LLC
Chambersburg PA
CBHW081359090726

47908CB00011B/2727